# The Poem is a Nomad

ALSO BY CAL KINNEAR:

*A Walk in Bardo*
*Shale Eyes*
*My Father's House*
*The Great Wheel: Zero the Un-Naming*

# The Poem is a Nomad

## Cal Kinnear

TAUROLOG / CHATWIN BOOKS
2018

ISBN 978-1-63398-055-6

A co-publication of Taurolog and Chatwin Books.
Copyright © Cal Kinnear, 2017-2018. No part of this book may be used or reproduced in any manner without written permission from the publishers, except in the context of reviews and short excerpts used in teaching.

Chatwin Books
Seattle, Washington
www.chatwinbooks.com

Taurolog Books
Vashon Island, Washington
calkinnear@gmail.com

Cover design and artwork, book production & author photo by Annie Brulé
Cover photo by Galyna Andrushko, Shutterstock
Book design by Cal Kinnear & Annie Brulé

# CONTENTS

| | |
|---|---|
| *Gone Hunting* | 5 |
| *The Winter Night Sings* | 9 |
| *What the Hive Says* | 25 |
| *Voices on the Way* | 39 |
| *Going Lost* | 45 |
| *The Voyage Through Books* | 57 |
| *Coming Home in the Dark* | 67 |
| About the Author | 79 |

*Gone Hunting*

WHERE is the poem
gone? Won't take a collar,
gone hiding out there. Everything's
owned.
Books,
imprisoned on shelves,
in glass-faced cabinets.
You buy. Or you get a card,
the kind that gets you
into the library. Or
the courthouse:
show your fingerprints, leave
your pocket knife in the tray.
Everything in here
is incarcerated. That's the law.
So where's the poetry?
It's out there, it's gone missing
and no search party
is going to find it.

To live is to want, and
so to seek the words for wanting,
its journey, and
the name for what will not be owned,
with the grief that attends.

*The Winter Night Sings*

THIS ANCIENT WANDERER, sleep-wrinkled
with endless dream, endless awakening,
an almost inaudible scented whisper
of enticement
on his breath.
With the faintest word he names
perplexity, intricacy, complicity, vertigo,
enchantment.

THE WIND over the roof is
the tongue of a glacier,
licking my house away a syllable at a time.
This night will not end.
I will never sleep again. A vigil
frail as the eyes of the oldest man.
Nothing to hold off freezing or fear.
Only a small lantern, flickering,
some red clay cups on a table,
a geranium on the window sill.
Anything is possible.

'MY HOUSE' I SAY, wanderer that I am.
How many years ago I set out.
At night, walls overwritten with yesterday.
Bed with wakefulness perched over the pillow.
A sigh in the dark.

THIS ROOM AND I,
constantly moving at the same speed,
and so we stay together
through the long nights.
The chair remains in the corner,
by the shelves of books.
The lamp casts its soft glow across
the toucan's portrait.
This lends a kind of security.
But the room itself rides some element
that shifts its course like a river.
Here on the desk is a basil leaf.
And hanging from the ceiling here is
a bubble of blue glass the ocean cast up.
And here is my grandfather
lying down for a nap
with a crossword puzzle
spread over him like a sheet.
And here. In this photograph,
I am the shadow you can just see.
No one in the world
looks like this anymore.

AND THIS CHAIR still holds
the same vanishment left
when a friend stood up, and
never came back. All souls
are travelling away from one another
at an immeasurable speed. They
spin in orbit with one another
with a gravity proportionate
to their distance apart.

How can I explain my fear?
Faceless thieves. I
have not seen them. They
have taken nothing.
I awake breathless and
light up the lantern.
Everything is here.
My clock. The picture of irises.
The other of two turtles.
My desk with its books and papers.
My pants and shirt draped over a chair.
My shoes. What is going missing,
slipping away so fast
it leaves me dizzy?
The ground under my feet
is in free fall and I'm falling
at the same speed.

THE WIND WENT CRASHING all night long,
and I could hear distant voices singing Gloria,
but when I looked out the window
there was no one. And why would anyone
go out on a night like this to sing?
So the Gloria lives somewhere
in the eddies of the wind like
a bee flying through amber.
Like a rose in a corona of ice.
Impossible. Unless
this Gloria is the hidden sanctuary
of winter night.

THE LAST SLANT SUNLIGHT
of a winter day prints
brilliant black leaves upon the wall.
Then they lie on, silent, invisible,
shadow within shadow, rippling softly
to hold against the current,
as the night tears by.

THE RED TILE TABLE in the kitchen
with its own small lantern.
It is the season to move slowly
and gather comfort.
Every face comes doubled with ghosts.
A smile is water. A hand holding a cup
is a crow's wing. Things move and cross,
bits of glass and mirrorings.
It's easy to fall down,
to lose the way, to forget.
It's all right. It's
the persistent motion of a dream
in a field without gravity. It's
the rising tide of hibernal sleep.

**There is a horizon**
around a black hole.
No one is quite sure what it's like.
A crater? A drain pipe?
Free fall into solitude.
My words all still with me.
And if I ask,
who is it answers?
It is you, only you,
a match struck
your voice written
in flickers of fire
and ash.
At the horizon,
crossing over takes
forever.

It's still at last,
at the bottom of a wan ocean of light,
what's left after a tsunami of night.
Like getting up after a long fever
with a stranger for a body.
And the wall of the room
is only there for as long as I watch it,
and if the kettle whistles from the kitchen,
it must be time to make tea.
And what am I to make of
these tiny glass creatures
that washed up and stayed?
A red heron.
A yellow horse.
A royal blue bull.

Names come to me like foxfire.
All my loved ones, the absent, my loss.
The soul-life swirling tight in the name.
Waving and guttering
up and down the trees,
a ghostly conflagration. They
speak themselves, they echo and fade.
Always the lament,
what all runs together roughly,
in beauty, in grief.
A battlefield, a lover's bed.
And excess beyond any story.
The force of the name
calling out
the tangled threads of the soul.
Time later to sort.

THERE ARE THINGS
I can't say to anyone
face to face.
I leave them like breath-prints
in the frost on the window.
A moment ago, it was dark,
the longest night of the year.
And now there are ducks,
sprouted like mushrooms
from sheer unruffled water.
A breeze blows down from the dawn.

*What the Hive Says*

AND THE DAY AT LAST I wake up
it begins again.
The hum of the bees scouting over the heather,
the smoke in the half-light,
the plash of water. My hunger
already knows who you are, singing softly.
We walk together about the room,
lovers in our first intimacy.
I say your names beginning with
sparrow and going on through grief to ember.
You are all the light I have to see by.
Go, I say, you can't ever stay.
It's my calling to keep forgetting you.

OCTOBER,
and still a few bees
walk upon the sage.
Flowers drowse all day
in the roaring light.
Bees are a haze of sound
over the meadow.
All that the flower has heard,
the bee dances
in its narrow cell.
There is no solitude deeper
than hunger,
the smoke that rises
from dreams.

OUT OF THE SMOKY AIR of dream
you come flying back.
You have to pace your floor,
no matter what hour, back and forth.
Your steps make a carpet of air,
weaving tongues out of the smoke.
Each step is a new world.
Hunger dances itself.

CELL AFTER CELL of the sacred hive.
A dust of pollen shaken from my skin.
The air is alive with tongues.
Everything that needs to say says
here. Anyone belongs here. Alone,
and not. This is the hive,
the breeding place of words.
But how did I come here?
Walking in circles, dreaming.

A WHOLE METROPOLIS of cells,
each the only one. The sleeper
folded up in the womb of sleep,
folded around the embryo
of himself dreaming.
The countless bees swarm,
bringing the names,
the words, the hum,
the pure white noise
embroidered
with threads of color.
A ferment of sound falling
through the whirlpool of an ear.
I am anyone,
my companions the voices
orbiting about me.

THE CELL CLOSES AND FOLDS.
The heat rises.
All the wide world
to be danced out
in a narrow pacing.
One step
and then another,
and then a turn,
over bare pages,
scar tissue printing
a chart of the ways,
one over another.
This is the way I walk,
this is it.
With precisely
this weave.
With precisely
this limp.

**ONE STEP**
and then another.
Sparks, match-flares.
Almost enough to see by.
The soles of my feet
know a design.
Walking on
fractured letters
they are criss-crossed
with scars.
The floor of the cell
is written and overwritten.
It's too late to scrub it clean.
The walking
is its own sense,
at any hour of the night,
in the absence of sleep.

THE DREAMER FALLS
deeper into his house.
The rain barrel by the porch
holds a broken reflection.
No one arrives at the door for weeks.
Nothing slows the chrysanthemums
in their rust and golden blooming.
The bees arrive
one by one
to walk the walls of their hive,
shrouded in a smoke of white noise
and sweetness.
A name calls itself out, unheard.
The moss-covered roof grows heavier.
A pheasant
picks the laces of an empty shoe,
tilts its head and glares.

No voice yet.
The walls are paper
and just out of reach.
The only sound now,
the small gray fall of rain
on still water.
An empty book
lies narrow and dark on the table.
Its covers are like two hands
pressed palm to palm
in a gesture of waiting.
Then I hear
the curled syllable of a name
like breathing in a flute.
The book stirs, opens.
There is a clatter of wings,
the sound of small feet
running. What is
inside, what is out?

It will come to me
when I least expect.
My name. My
true name.
I will be sitting
on the edge of my bed,
tying my shoe. Reaching
in my pocket for a coin.
Ah, of course, how utterly right.
An inheritance, a hand-me-down,
and an apparition.
It explains nothing. It
tells everything.
But then every word is a name.

**What does this sound like,**
to be called? To hear
my name spoken
for the first time,
to know it,
to answer, Yes?
My name, the one
I've never heard before.
And know what it means,
meaning me. Now I've heard it,
it's like a phrase of music,
like what a river says
diving among rocks.
It covers me
like the fox-reek of a dark den.
Goes-a-long-way-alone.
Dreams-the-secrets-of-water.
Sleeps-with-the-foxes.
Whatever name, it matters.
Now I know where
I will go away to die.

*Voices on the Way*

**These words,** these names.
They have nothing to tell,
no report, no news.
A small flower, intensely blue,
grows in a granite cleft.
There is no map, no trail.
At dawn and twilight
I give myself up
to listening.
I live this far away to come near
the silence of words. I listen
through the rustling of birds and wind.
Wax, I hear, and
horseshoe, tin, ochre, chime,
languid, rapt. I think
I am learning to be a song.

A VALLEY as long as a day's walking,
granite and small grasses and
nowhere anything but wind and
a single tiny speckled egg. And
maybe only there at last
where there is so little to say,
and no one to say it to,
will I begin to hear what
the names have to say.
A song whorled through
the throat of the wind.

The silent, midnight hunters
are out there, each
with his name clenched
in his teeth, full
of a sharp hunger.
Nothing but
the energy of names
tracking over the ground.
I sit by the bank of a river
indistinguishable from a stone
and listen to their silent calling.
Listen. They are hungry
with an inexpungeable law.
They love one another
with ancient loyalties.
If I keep still,
they pretend to ignore me,
as if I were not the prey.

*Going Lost*

From that jagged ridge of stone
tufted with clumps of mountain goat fur,
the mountain plunged
sheer on either side thousands of feet.
No one could ever sleep there.
You could either jump,
or climb back down.
Or stay on without a trace—
vast, vertiginous, light-scarred,
serrate, dumb.

A LONG TIME SINCE
I stood by the sea.
The gray roaring
mixed with
snarls of white.
Where there are
names to listen for.
Where I stood
naked in the wash.
Sea-gray
out from shore,
swathed in fog
at the world's edge.
Turnstone, sandpiper,
geoduck and
the auger hole of a moon snail.
The spindrift
off the crests of the breakers.
A trawler in the offing
wallowing by.
Clouds tearing themselves
on the cypresses
at the top of the long clay banks.
A single sound, that

gray washing everywhere.
The name of the sea whispers
in my room, and I feel
the tug of the tide.

I am here as if I were inside.
If I move, walls move,
a curtain shakes in the wind,
a woman mutters in her sleep.
Three wolves pass
on my right hand,
smoky, invisible.
A small lizard climbs
over the knuckle of my thumb.
An owl cries once,
long and ululant.
Everything is
coming into being at once.
Word by word,
I turn more animal.

I KNOW
just where he is
under the grass
where I walk,
though
there's not a mark.
The boy
who had to die
for my grief.
The boy
who had to die
so I could believe
he was possible.
That his beauty
was possible,
with his legs like
wind through the grass,
the butterflies
dancing out of his eyes
and his hair
the bees plaited
with honey.
I have heard him,
I have heard him,

murmuring
his name to himself,
like rain
washing over the roof.

Maybe I'm only doing something simple
like washing my face. My hands are happy.
They go on with what they're doing
and forget all about me. Suddenly
there's no one here, no one about to speak,
No one who wanted to wash his face.
The water continues falling, so certain of itself.
My hands rise again, streaming water,
out of nowhere.

RECROSSING THE ROOM
how many times,
without ever reaching the edge.
Listening for
the small beckon of voices
from within the close air.
They speak of this and that,
of the *olor* of orange flowers,
of surf, of sweated skin,
of the circumpolar flights of albatrosses,
of fallow fields
where the snow falls all night.
These things blaze
the faintest trail over
a folded geography,
everywhere discontinuous,
everywhere leaving
word of themselves.

How light they are,
each word a mix
of flame and levity,
about to vanish like
the steam-whorls
above a cup of coffee.
Look
what I've brought inside—
sky and earth,
hail from the belly
of a thunderstorm,
the cries of countless geese
from the dark lake.
A fox.
Yes, you see,
it's night inside, and sleep,
and dream.
Saying dissolves.
All weighted things await
the comeliness of words.
Here is gaiety and grief, music,
and the passage back to light.

*The Voyage Through Books*

Home again.
The walls are in tatters.
The light of stars sifts in.
I sit in the profoundest silence,
listening to nothing, as it
sings and sings and sings.
Memory after memory
drumming on the floor
asking to be let in.

LATE NIGHT in my library.
Books all around me,
the silence and
patience of their voices.
A book opens.
What care to embalm the voice.
A dark bed of velvet
within a leather case.
Scent of wax and lemon oil.
The dark wood glows.
The letters bristle and writhe,
guarding something.
The page is alive with sparks.
I feel the heat of watching
rise to a sweat. There is
no air, and I
will have to read anyway.
All reading is translation,
and I know no Hindi, no Aleut.
The words lie there in their silence,
so beautiful, so enchanting,
so exquisitely formed.

A THING LEFT BEHIND,
like a staff of cedar
ornamented with
flicker feathers and
mother of pearl.
Left behind,
an urgency. Listen.
Knotted air, only
sudden delicate knots
sketched in the air.
The intricate
tangle of them.
Every knot
is a name.
The nighthawks
call to one another
overhead.

**The seven hundred year old cedar**
grows from the fallen body of a thousand
    year old cedar.
In the deep gravures of its bark
grow whole populations of ants and wasps
    and worms.
A coffin is a closed thing. It says something has
    finished,
driving the nail home.
Francis Bacon said
    *Sometimes a man's shadow is more in the room than he is,*
and painted it.
Emily Dickinson put away her poems in a box.
It was only a year ago I found in a new book
the fifteen hundred year old poems of Vidya.
There are never-dying things
lying sheathed like tempered blades
in rare silk in a dark drawer.

LOOK,
here is a book of pictures shut up,
the outlandish oases of the world,
arrived at out of desert
and unrelenting sun.
Watchful eyes,
a monotony of walking,
a desire completed and
abandoned again in a picture.
A life shut up, finished
in the closing of a book.
A call. 'Come with me
into yourself.'

It's no secret, though
it comes from so hidden a place
it feels like one.
I tell what I hear. These words
travelling at the speed of
their own incandescence
take lifetimes to arrive.
I watch the ragged streaming clouds
part a moment to reveal
the full sail of the moon.
This is only one syllable of the name
I am trying to write.

EACH NIGHT the sleeper on the pillow
grows drier and fainter.
An old photo is
beginning to give up its image.
Sparrows visit daily,
squabbling over the crumbs of bread.
I keep a handful of dark earth
in my pocket.
I pick the voice of an old friend
out of an envelope, a word at a time.
It tastes faintly of iron.
The walls glimmer
with the golden tattering of old leaves.
There is a music
in the shadow of the room that is
the color of rust and oak.

'F*INIS*,' I read,
and close the book,
put it away,
turn out the light,
lock the door, and
begin to fall through
the soft ringing
in my ears into
the absolution of sleep.
Each syllable
slips away, a cat
with its night-eyes,
to hunt, all the way
to the last syllable of
my uttermost name,
a drone
in the throat of
a dream organ pipe.

*Coming Home in the Dark*

One after another they come in,
shaking light from them
like drops of water. It is
the moment before night.
The light is autumnal,
distracted by
each dancing dust mote.
It collects where it can,
on the cobalt rim of a glass,
on a cat's eye, on the blade
of a ceremonial sword.
And the lunar work begins.
The cheese glows
in the middle of its savor.
The violin slumbering
in its case of velvet,
throbs with dances.
The tremble of a sigh.
The memory of lights turns
within itself, within
its sleep, passing through
the depths of a still mirror.

ALL NIGHT LONG the moon
falls dizzily through the sky.
Recumbent angel
in the waters of sleep.
Moon of dark wine.
Angel of still water,
wrinkled by
the night stirring of bees.

THE WORDS LIE under my tongue
like the stones a night river
pours over. The shades of grey,
the riffles, the drone. We
meet in the race
below the point of the gravel bar.
We speak together
in an indistinguishable voice,
within the roaring.

**OPEN THE DOOR,** but carefully.
A few haven't yet fallen asleep.
An angel on the edge of sleep
trembles its wings. Inside
has the hush of a root cellar.
If you walk you will get lost.
If you sit you will turn to stone.
Listen. At midnight the tide crests.
For the space of a breath
time stops. The voices come
all in a rush, scented with mint
and bog water. It's like
a million salmon vaulting
toward the headwaters.
Every word is an omen,
a divination, a sorcery,
a talisman. Where do you think
words came from, already
knowing so surely
who they are? Open
the door. Do.

Time-out.
They hover side-by-side, as
they have always known how to do,
sometimes
a few words, sometimes
silent. They edge forward,
knowing the way
always only just as
it enters them, calling them,
knowing them
by names they don't yet know.
There will be no rest in the end,
no spawn. Only
the light rising
in the skin, the gradual
reddening,
the late flame
before night.

THE SONG is not
written or read.
It is borne. It is
inside the word
rising toward
the surface.
The song is a nomad
the bee out of
a hundred miles of air
entering
the haunted pueblo,
to pace out
its blessing
on the floor.
Hive hum,
honey smoke,
souls in dream pass
through the walls.
A calligraphy
of breath, a tent,
an ark.

A THOUSAND CANDLES
in a space dwindling
toward a point.
The heat
of all those bodies
pressed together
in celebration.
The voices
in their intricate
pitchings
rising toward light—
blue first, then red,
then white,
reaching
the concentration
of a star.

TIME SPILLS in the slow cold arc of the moon.
It lies in lakes across the floor.
The spawn of frogs and lizards
stir among golden carp in the shallows.
Silver leaves sift like snow down the air,
stirring the limbs of dreamers floating
just above the surface, their eyes
soft and wide with wonder. Bridges, stairways,
the confused murmur of bare feet running,
then the utter silence of two in the morning.
A single white egret stands on the bank,
with his immutable, imperishable golden eye.

*Cal Kinnear lives on the island of the Swiftwater People in the Salish Sea.*

www.ingramcontent.com/pod-product-compliance
Lightning Source LLC
Chambersburg PA
CBHW060539080526
44586CB00012B/797